FEARLESS JOHN
The Legend of John Beargrease

by Kelly Emerling Rauzi
illustrated by Mila Horak

Published by
Singing River Publications, Inc.
PO Box 72
Ely, MN 55731-0072
www.singingriverpublications.com

Author: Kelly Emerling Rauzi
Artwork: Mila Horak
Design & Layout: Kelly Rauzi & Mila Horak

Printed in Canada.

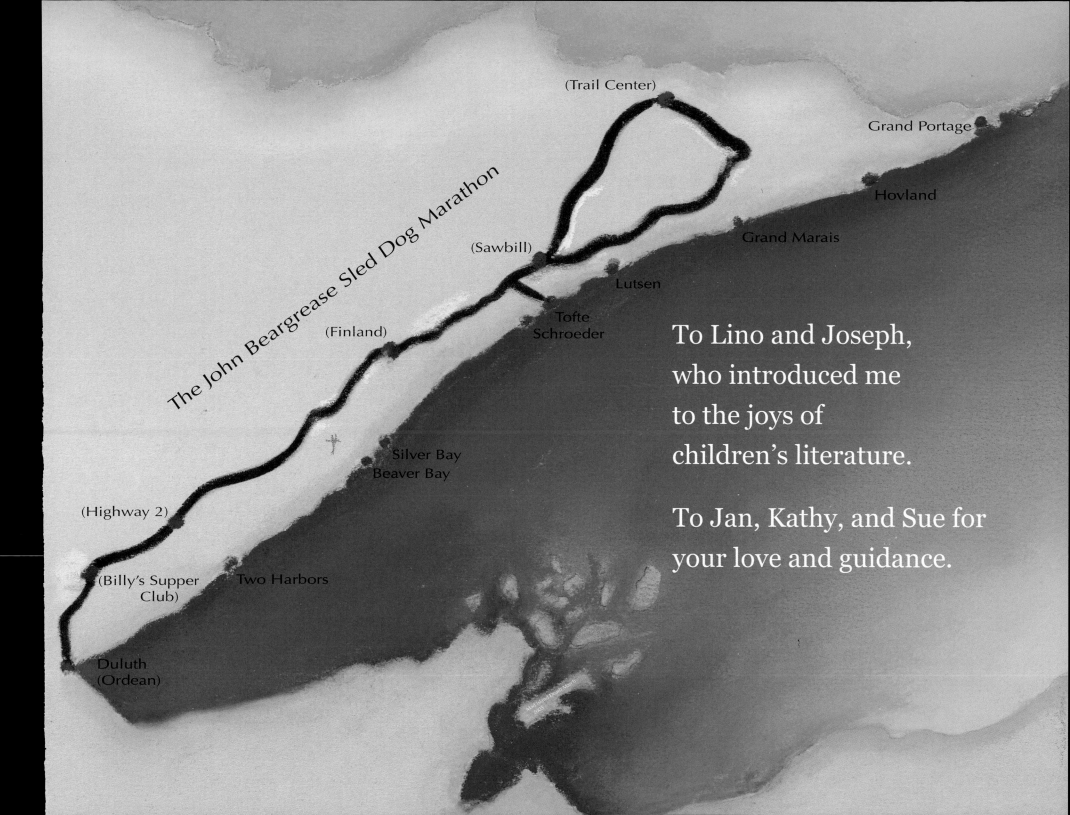

The John Beargrease Sled Dog Marathon

(Trail Center)

Grand Portage

Hovland

Grand Marais

(Sawbill)

Lutsen

Tofte
Schroeder

(Finland)

Silver Bay
Beaver Bay

(Highway 2)

(Billy's Supper
Club)

Two Harbors

Duluth
(Ordean)

To Lino and Joseph,
who introduced me
to the joys of
children's literature.

To Jan, Kathy, and Sue for
your love and guidance.

D URING THE WINTER on the North Shore of Lake Superior, the constellation Orion the hunter appears on the eastern horizon and swings steadily through the southern sky. Orion and his faithful dogs, *Canis Major* (the big dog) and *Canis Minor* (the little dog), watch over the deep, cold lake and the people who live in the Sawtooth Mountains along the shore.

Winters in the Sawtooth Mountains are long and hard. Some years frequent storms bring heavy snows and deep, white pillows of flakes that pile on rooftops and block the view from low windows. Other years the snow is sparse, leaving patches of land exposed and frozen in the raw winds that whip off the lake.

People look forward to the snowy years. When Orion and his dogs appear in November, it is time to wax cross-country skis and pull snowshoes out of storage. The local mushers prepare their dog teams and sleds for travel on backwoods trails.

As soon as the snow falls, dog teams train
for the running of the John Beargrease
Sled Dog Marathon.   Each January this 375
mile race follows a challenging trail through
the wilderness between Duluth
and Grand Marais.

Proud old white
pines bow respectfully
to the racers as they press
forward—through all kinds of
weather. The dogs run during storms
that drive hard bits of snow into the faces
of the mushers. Some nights the sleds glide
over hard-packed snow glowing in moonlight.
All teams race in memory of John Beargrease,
the North Shore's most hardy and faithful mail carrier.

JOHN BEARGREASE lived during the latter half of the 1800's. He was the eldest son of the Anishinaabe Chief Mokquabemmette— Chief Beargrease. Not much is known about John's mother. She likely was of French-Canadian descent, a relative of the Voyageurs—rugged explorers who traveled in giant canoes through the Great Lakes and waters along the American-Canadian border, trading manufactured goods for furs from the Native Americans. From his parents, John Beargrease inherited the characteristics of leadership, adventure, and fearlessness.

As a grown man John stood over six feet tall. He was lean and wiry-strong. He made his home in a wigwam at the mouth of the Beaver River with his wife Louise and their many children.

Louise must have been a strong
woman—and independent—
because John was often not at home.
Most of his time was spent outdoors
traveling long distances with his dogs
and his gun along the wild North Shore.

Beargrease first used the Old Dog Trail, a narrow footpath that connected Duluth to Port Arthur, Ontario as a boy. He easily tracked the animals that live in the boreal forest. He hunted and checked traps with his brothers. He made his own bows, arrows, and canoes.

Beargrease was widely known for his skills as a hunter and woodsman. One time, while out hunting with a friend, John had only two bullets for his gun. Suddenly three deer bounded across a clearing and disappeared into thick brush. As hard as John's friend strained his eyes, he could not see the deer. John aimed his gun into the woods and fired two shots. Minutes later, the men were cleaning two deer to bring home to their hungry families.

With admiration and disbelief, the friend asked John how he could have seen the animals well enough to have aimed so accurately.

John said, "When I can't see the deer, I can smell them."

As the Beargrease brothers worked
their traps and hunted up and down the shore,
they began to carry mail along the trail.
It was as a mail carrier that John Beargrease
became legendary. The people called
him **Fearless John.**

For nearly a quarter of a century, when
most people in the United States were receiving
letters by rail or by Pony Express, Fearless John
delivered the mail by foot, boat, and sled.

Families anticipated his arrival.
In the winter children waited to hear
the bells on the dogs' collars jingle as Beargrease
pulled into delivery points on his sled. The noise of the bells
protected Fearless John and his team from attacks by hungry wolves.

When the team arrived in town, a crowd gathered around Fearless John to hear the news: "The Eliasens of Hovland have delivered a healthy baby boy! The ice is eight inches thick on the bays north of Grand Marais! The Berglunds are planning for the wedding of their daughter Alma to Andrew Hedstrom next fall!"
Everyone relied on Fearless John to keep them connected to a larger world.

And as legend has it, Fearless John Beargrease never let the
people of the North Shore down. During the warm months
he hiked the Old Dog Trail, tolerating biting black flies,
mosquitos, summer heat, and rain. He climbed into
and out of muddy ravines and steep gorges and
crossed rivers flowing over slippery ledge rock.

During the winter, when Orion and his dogs dominated
the night sky, Fearless John guided his own dogs and
toboggan-like sled just off Lake Superior's shore.
When it was possible, he cut travel time by crossing
the unpredictable, heaving and shifting ice
covering the bays. Alone and with his life
at great risk, Fearless John sometimes
carried nearly 700 pounds on his sled.

Besides the mail, his winter load included snowshoes, tobacco, a rifle, and a knife. He carried dried meats and ate other foods hunted and gathered along the way. Fearless John didn't waste much time cooking meals or sleeping, even in the coldest weather, so he often pulled into towns along his route looking for a bed, a meal, and relief from frostbite.

Like all good mushers and their teams, Fearless John and his dogs developed a strong bond of dependency and respect. When they got stuck on the trail, he shared food and comfort with his dogs. They nestled into hollows together, keeping warm and dry while winter storms swirled around them. As they ran, Fearless John reassured his team with a coaxing, rhythmic voice. "Hi! Yi! Yi!" he yelled, and his dogs pulled.

His team trusted him and ran hard for him. According to legend, Fearless John clocked his fastest time between Two Harbors and Grand Marais with only four dogs, covering a distance of nearly 80 miles in 28 hours! Mushers with larger teams in today's John Beargrease Sled Dog Marathon struggle to match this time.

Towards the end of Fearless John's mail carrying days, travel on the North Shore became less treacherous. The Old Dog Trail, or North Shore Trail, was widened and graded. Bridges were built, making travel by horse and carriage or sleigh possible. Beargrease began using a steel land barge to carry the winter mail. Pulled by a draft horse, this huge sled could transport nearly a ton of cargo. Mail by dogsled had seen its last days. One has to wonder if Fearless John missed those quiet times on the trail and the frozen lake with his faithful dogs pulling a smaller sled full of letters and packages.

In the spring of 1899 John Beargrease delivered his last load of mail. He then retired to the Grand Portage Indian Reservation, where he lived for the next decade. In 1910 Fearless John performed a final act of courage: he ventured out on Lake Superior during

a fierce storm to rescue a fellow mail carrier. Godfrey Montferrand was caught in a Mackinaw boat tossing about in frigid, rolling waves near Grand Portage.

Fearless John rowed out into danger and managed to push Montferrand and his boat to shore before hypothermia's frozen sluggishness overtook the men's limbs and left them helpless. While Montferrand survived the accident, Fearless John was not so lucky.

After the rescue, John Beargrease suffered from tuberculosis, and eventually he died.

THE GREAT MEMORY of Fearless John Beargrease survives in a rugged and adventurous way of life on the North Shore of Lake Superior. Like Fearless John, many residents enjoy hunting and fishing and take extended trips into the back country—by foot or canoe or dogsled.

When Orion and his faithful dogs appear on November's eastern horizon and cold weather settles over the shore, preparations for the annual running of the John Beargrease Sled Dog Marathon begin.

The mushers who compete in this race embark upon a meaningful journey. Each winter they run with their own faithful dogs through the Sawtooth Mountains, following the spirit of Fearless John along a route that once belonged to him.

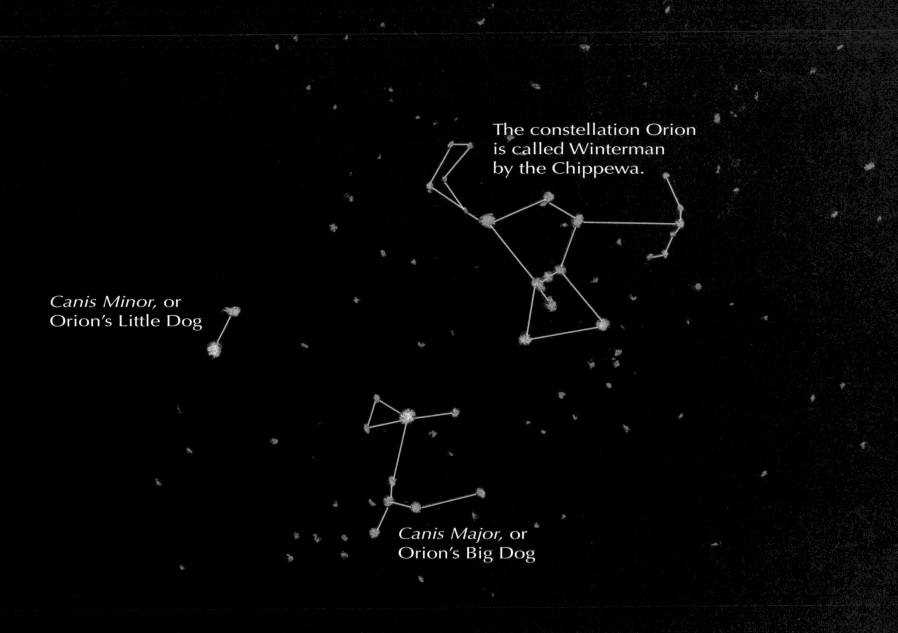

The constellation Orion is called Winterman by the Chippewa.

Canis Minor, or Orion's Little Dog

Canis Major, or Orion's Big Dog

Bibliography

Cameron, Don. *Keeper of the Town: Short Stories*. Superior, WI:
Savage Press, 1996. 83 - 89.

Dwan, Dennis. "Growth of the Postal System on the North Shore."
Minnesota Historical Society Manuscript Collection, 1933.

The Legend of John Beargrease. 17 September 2004
<http://www.beargrease.com>.

Raff, Willis H. *Pioneers in the Wilderness*. Grand Marais: Cook County
Historical Society, 1981.

Schiller, Emily. Sled Dogs and Mushers. 17 September 2004
<http://www.emily.net/~schiller/mushing.html>.

Sivertson, Howard. *Tales of the Old North Shore: Paintings and
Companion Stories*. Duluth: Lake Superior Port Cities, 1996.

Two Harbors Centennial Commission. "The Legend of John
Beargrease." *Two Harbors - 100 Years*. Two Harbors: Lake County
Historical Society, 1983.

Williams, Elise Sonja. "Homesteading on the North Shore." Utica/
Omaha, NE: Houchen Bindery L & D, 1975. (Obtained from the
Iron Range Research Center, Chisholm, MN)

Acknowledgements

We would like to thank the following people and organizations for their generous help with the production of this book:

Sue Robinson, Betsy Bowen, Christopher Rauzi, Jan and Kathy Horak, I.S.D. #166 Cook County Schools, Jane Gellner, John Engelking, Tigg at CPL Imaging of Duluth, Christine Moroni, Michael Wood, Sivertson Gallery, Rita and Henry Wehsler, Nick Jagunich, Abbey Hudler, Connie Wilson, Don and Michelle Emerling, Tom and Sandy Kemp, Mr. Oliver and Mrs. Elizabeth Bobseine, Craig Horak's Tire and Auto Lodge, Judy Peterson, Andrew J. Prokop, the staff at Betsy Bowen's Studio, the Angry Trout Cafe, Shelby Anderson, and the John Beargrease Race Committee.